The Best Ever Face Painting Kit

BY JACQUELINE RUSSON

THUNDER BAY
P·R·E·S·S

For Thomas, Samuel and Harriet

Published in 1995 by
Thunder Bay Press
Advanced Marketing Services, Inc.
Book Division
5880 Oberlin Drive, Suite 400
San Diego, CA 92121

Planned and produced by
Andromeda Oxford Limited
11-15 The Vineyard
Abingdon
Oxon OX14 3PX

Make-up, costumes and accessories: Jacqueline Russon
Make-up assistant: Charlotte Russon
Photographer: David Johnson
Designer: Kit Johnson
Illustrator: Peter Geissler

With special thanks to: Alex, Amy, Dominique, Emma, Glenn, Hailey, Harriet, Heidi, Jennifer, Jonathan, Matthew, Michael, Richard, Robert, Ruby, Sophie

ISBN 1-57145-060-2
Printed in England

CONTENTS

INTRODUCTION

Have you ever had your face painted? Wouldn't you like to try it yourself? Now, with this ***BEST EVER FACE PAINTING KIT***, you can paint faces at home or at a friend's, and have great fun trying out the many ideas you'll find in this book.

WHAT YOU NEED

The five basic colors of paint that you need are included with this kit. They are water-based, and will wash off with soap and water. At the beginning of each design, you are shown what colors to mix to make any other colors you will need. You will soon learn how much of each color to mix together to make the new color. Add black to darken a color and white to lighten a color, unless you are shown otherwise. You could also buy additional colors such as gold and silver. Some of the designs in the book show you the effects that these colors can achieve. You will need a sponge and brushes to apply the paints, jars or saucers in which to mix the paints, a water jar to clean the brushes, tissues to mop any spillages and wipe clean the brushes, a towel to cover your model, and a hairband to keep hair off the face.

Costumes

You can buy many accessories from costume stores. In addition, you could try places like garage sales, and charity stores. You will also find instructions for making costumes in the book.

Extras

To follow are various other make-up items you can use. The stencils are included in the kit. The others are available at costume, make-up and some toy stores. Use only products that are intended for face painting, and do not go too near the eyes with them.

Stencils can be used to paint all sorts of shapes onto your faces.
Stars and sequins can either be applied to wet make-up, or by using a special make-up glue called spirit gum.
Make-up glitter can be bought loose or as a gel.
Hair coloring can be applied with the face paints or with special hair spray.

IMPORTANT SAFETY NOTES

- **All the paints sold with this kit have passed safety regulations. However, always test the paints on your wrist before using them, and if you get any reaction or irritation from the paints, stop using them immediately, and wash them off.**
- **Never drink the paints.**
- **Never apply the paints over open cuts or sores.**
- **Do not use the paints if you suffer from a skin allergy of any kind.**
- **Take extra care when painting near the eyes. Never put paints directly into the eyes.**
- **If you use any extras, be sure that they are intended for face painting.**

TECHNIQUES

Here are a few basic techniques to help you. Before you begin, shake the pots, make sure that your equipment is clean, and rinse your brush or sponge after painting with one color and before applying a new color. Squeeze any excess water from the sponge before using it. Let each color dry before applying the new color.

Applying a base color

Face painting usually begins with a base color. First, dip your sponge into the color you want to apply. Then, wipe or dab the sponge around the face and over the eyelids and lips. Ask your model to look up, and carefully dab the base under the eyes. Make sure that your model's eyes are closed when painting very close to them.

Blending

Blending is when the outline of one color is softly mixed into the edge of another color. To achieve this effect, let the first color dry, then apply the second color. Using a dry sponge, gently dab the two colors together where they meet.

Using a brush

Hold your brush as you would a normal paint brush. First, dip the brush into the paint. Use a thin brush to outline a design or to paint on any small or detailed shapes. You can vary the size and thickness of the line depending on how hard you press. Use a thicker brush for larger areas. Apply several layers of paint to achieve a denser color.

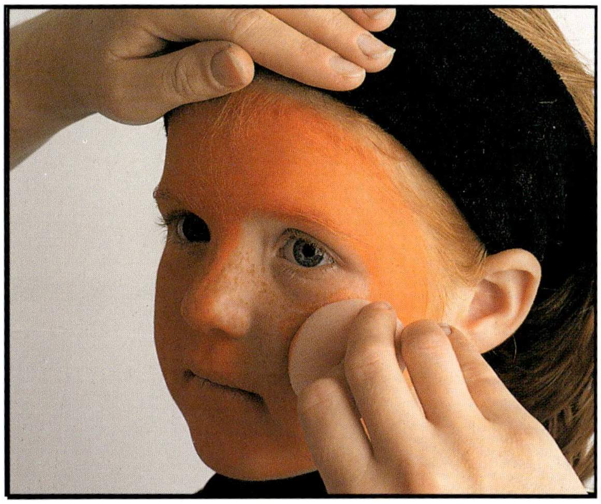

APPLYING A BASE COLOR

BLENDING

USING A BRUSH

DOZY DOG

COLOR MIX

1 Paint a white muzzle down the middle of the face and a white spot around each eye. Paint the rest of the face brown. Paint on two black eyebrows.

2 Paint your dog a red tongue. Paint the end of the nose black, and then a line from the nose to the top lip. Paint black whisker dots on the muzzle and stripes around the face.

FLUFFY RABBIT

COLOR MIX

To make **EARS AND HOOD** you will need:
Brown fur fabric * white fur fabric * wire * headband * glue * scissors * needle * thread

1 To make a hood, cut a rectangle from the fabric 20 inches long and 10 inches wide. Fold the fabric over. Stitch down one side of the fabric.

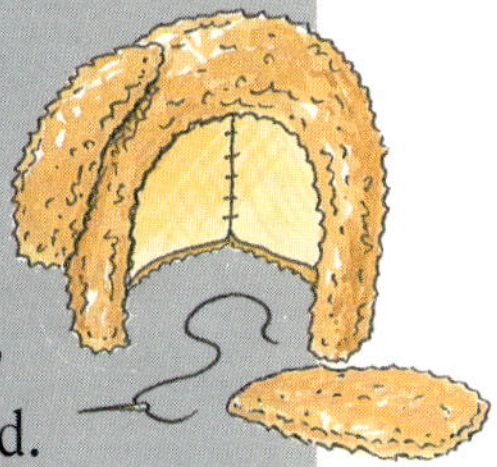

2 For the **DOG**, cut four ear shapes from the brown fabric. Glue two of them together. Repeat this with the other two ear shapes. Sew the ears to the top of the hood.

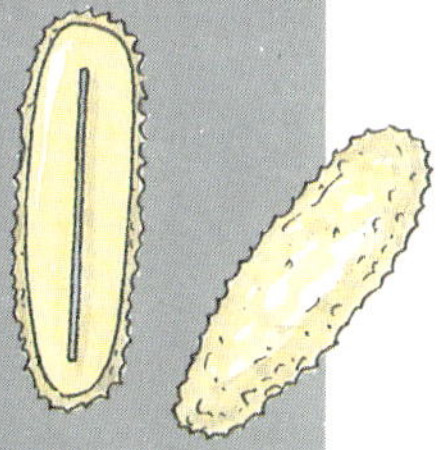

3 For the **RABBIT**, cut four ear shapes from the white fabric. Glue a piece of wire down the middle of two of the ear shapes, and glue a second ear shape on top.

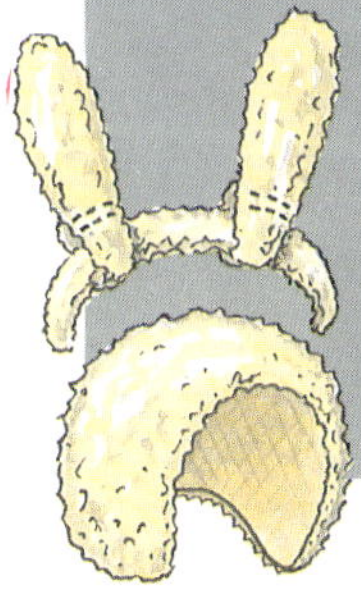

4 For the **RABBIT**, cover the headband with white fabric. Stitch the bottom of the ears around it. Wear the headband on top of the hood.

1 Apply a white base with a damp sponge. Using a fairly dry sponge, blend gray above the top lip. Paint a gray arch over each eye, and a black eyebrow above each arch.

2 Paint on two red cheeks, and smudge them with a dry sponge. Paint a black nose, and a black line from the nose to the mouth. Still using the black, outline two long teeth. Fill the teeth in with white. Add the whisker dots and whiskers.

EXOTIC BIRDS

COLOR MIX

BIRD OF PARADISE

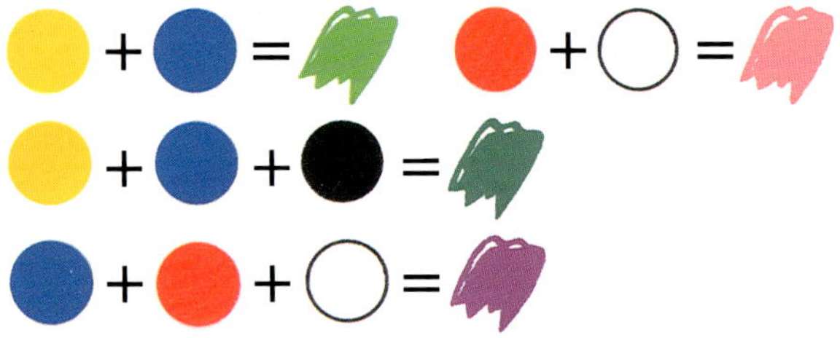

TROPICAL BIRD

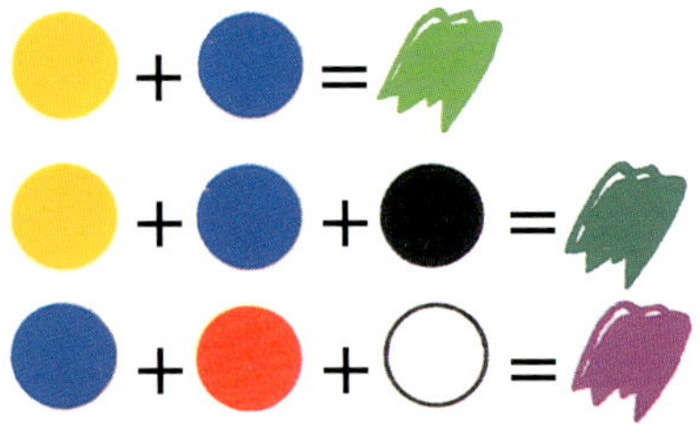

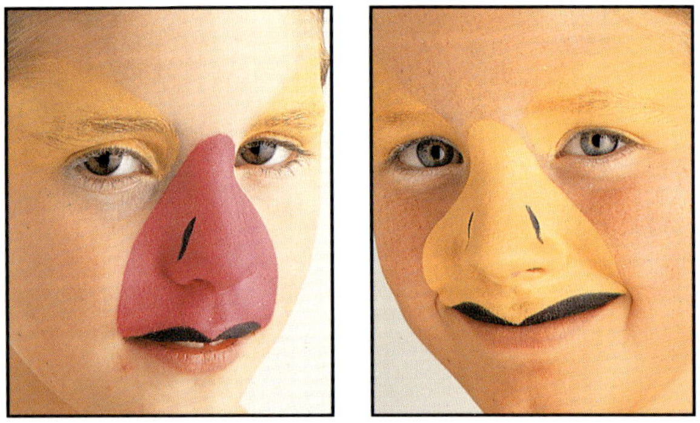

1 Paint a beak shape over the nose, using pink for the **BIRD OF PARADISE** and yellow for the **TROPICAL BIRD**. Outline the top lip in black, and paint a small black line on either side of the nose to give your bird nostrils. Paint over the eyelids and eyebrows with yellow.

2 Paint dark green feathers all around the face and up onto the forehead.

3 For the **BIRD OF PARADISE**, add purple, light green and pink feathers. For the **TROPICAL BIRD**, add purple, light green and red feathers. Sprinkle on green glitter.

Wrap a black feathery scarf around the **BIRD OF PARADISE**, and a pink feathery scarf around the **TROPICAL BIRD**.

MUMMY AND DRACULA

COLOR MIX

MUMMY

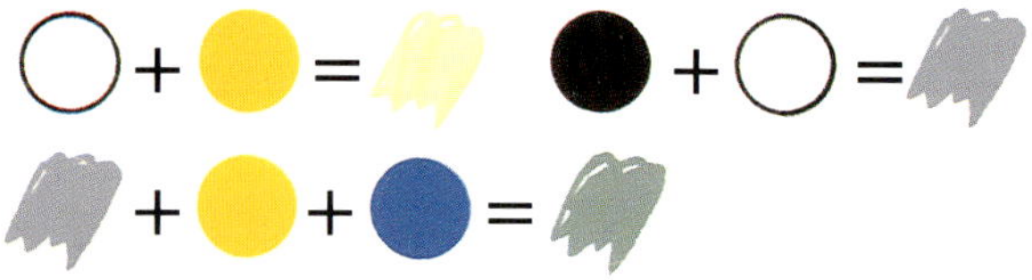

DRACULA

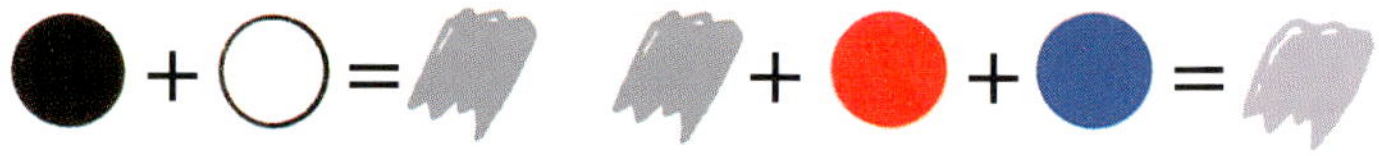

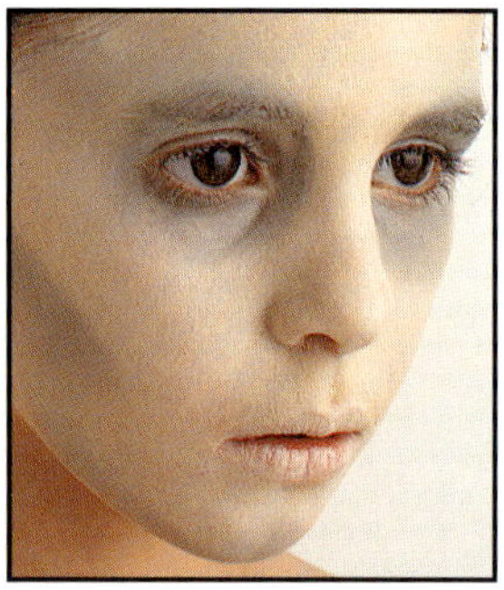

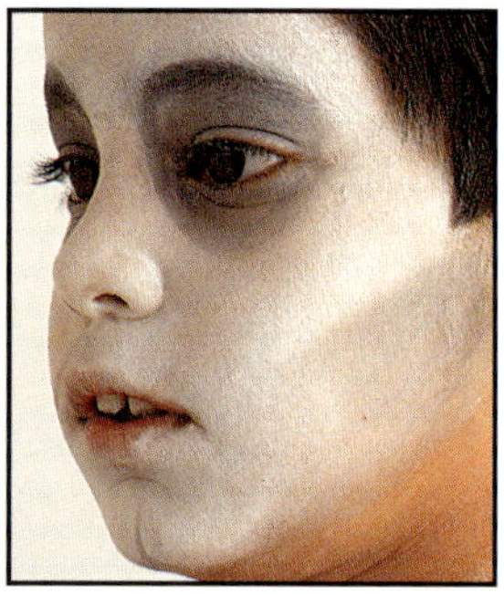

1 Apply a cream base for the **MUMMY**. Apply a white base for **DRACULA**. Blend gray around the eyes, under the cheek bones, the sides of the forehead and the chin.

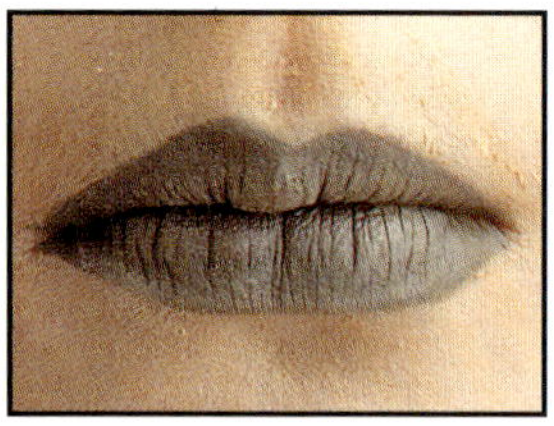

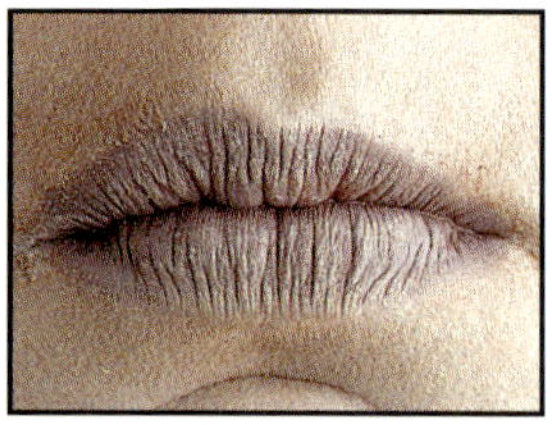

2 Paint the **MUMMY'S** lips a greenish gray, and **DRACULA'S** lips a purplish gray. Sponge some white on top of the lips to make them look wrinkly.

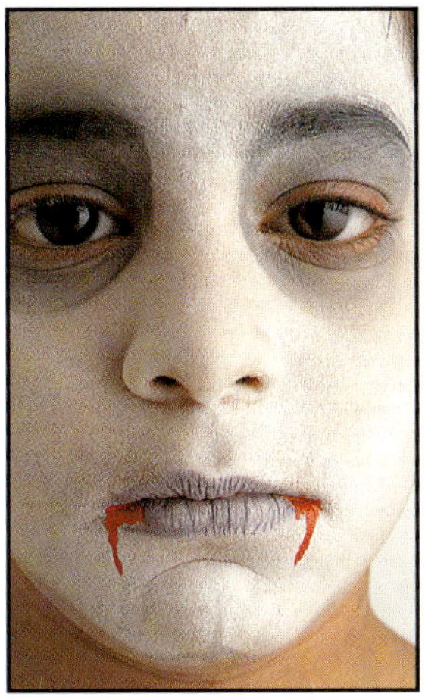

3 Paint a red line around the top and bottom of the eyes and smudge it with a dry sponge. Darken the eyebrows with black paint. Paint drops of blood from the corner of **DRACULA'S** mouth to make him look really scary.

To make a **DRACULA HAT** you will need:
Black card * black ribbon * glue * scissors

1 From some of the card, make a tube wide enough to fit around your head.

2 Snip all the way around each end of the tube to make tabs. Fold the top tabs inwards, and the bottom tabs outwards.

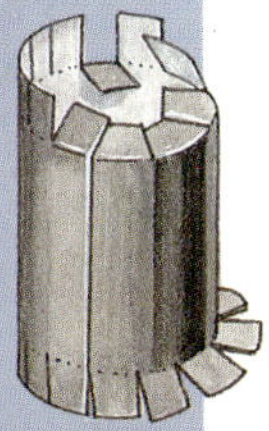

3 To make a brim for your hat, cut out a circle from the card that is about 4 inches wider than the tube. Cut a hole from the middle of the circle, making sure that it is as wide as the tube.

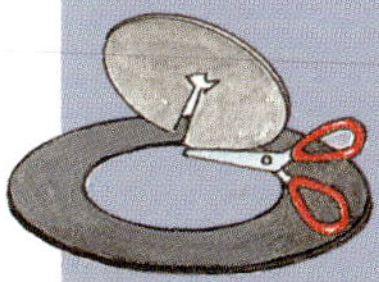

4 Push the brim to the bottom of the tube. Glue it to the tabs.

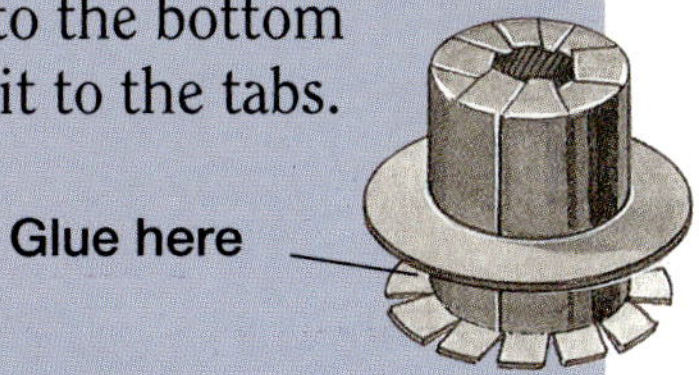

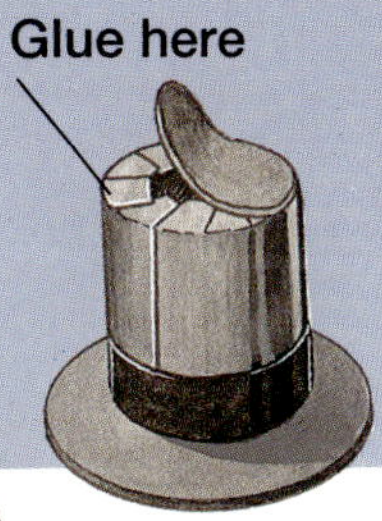

5 Cut out a circle to fit the top end of the tube, and glue it down. Glue a piece of black ribbon around your hat.

MISS BUTTERFLY

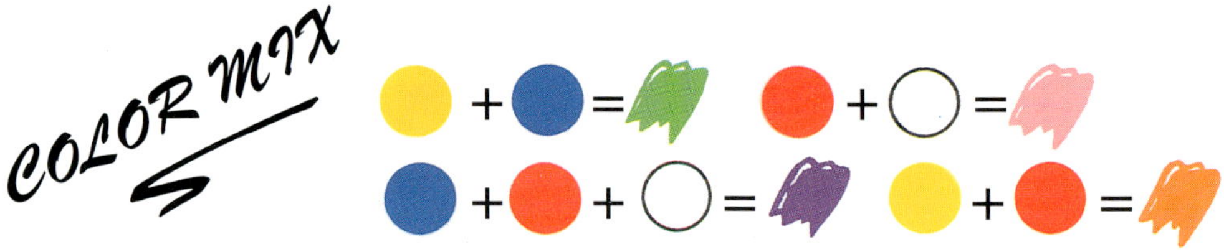

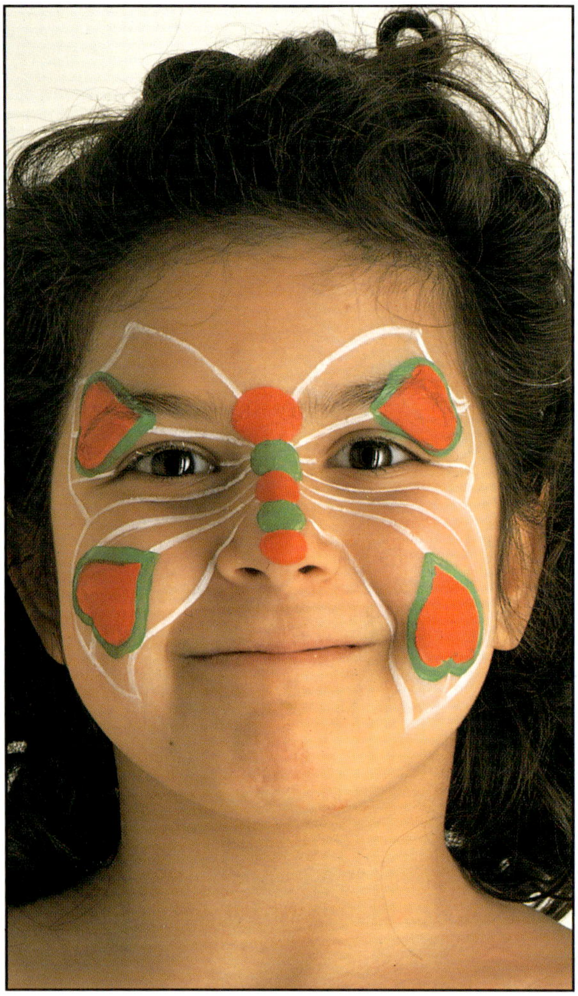

1 Using the tip of your brush and white paint, outline the shape of the butterfly. Fill in the red and green sections.

2 Fill in the pink sections of the butterfly, and then the purple and orange sections. Carefully paint on purple antennae.

3 Paint on some bright yellow dots to complete the butterfly.

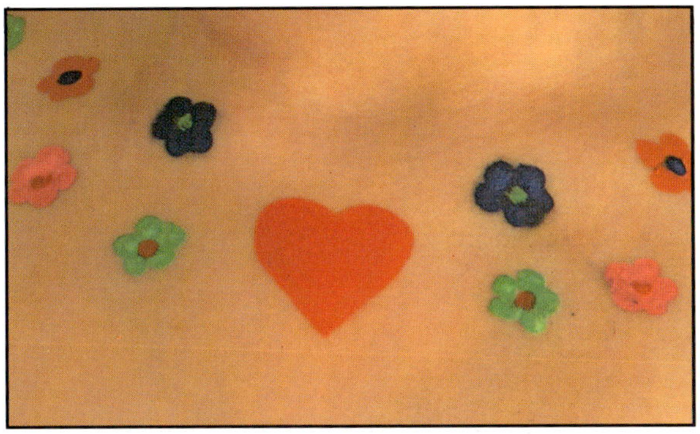

4 To make the necklace, paint a red heart just below the middle of the neck, and then paint flowers each side of it. Add a blob of paint to the middle of each flower.

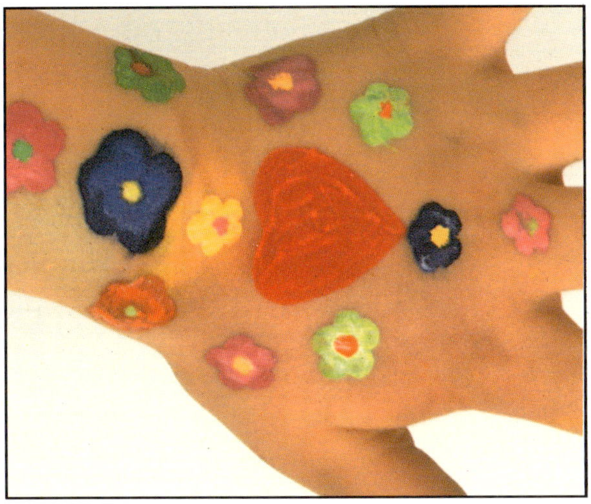

HANDY ART
Paint hearts and flowers onto your own or your friend's hands. You could try all sorts of other shapes.

WACKY WIZARD

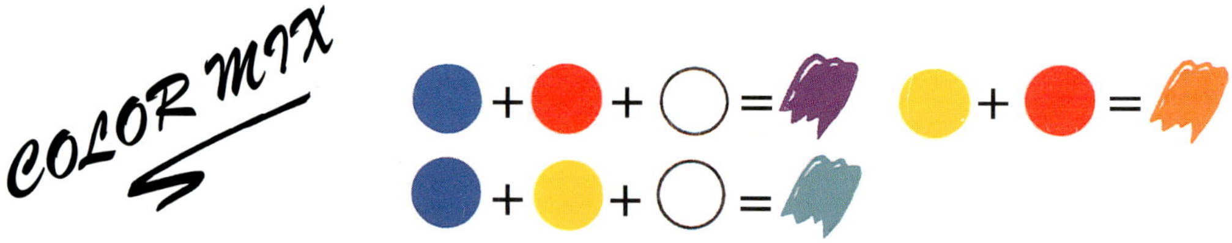

1 Sponge a white base over the face. Paint turquoise over the eyelids and under the eyes. Then paint purple over the eyebrows.

2 Using the tip of your brush, paint pointed black eyebrows above the purple sections.

3 Paint moons and suns onto the cheeks. You could use the colors shown in the color mix, or mix some of your own.

4 Paint the lips turquoise. You could add glitter around the eyelids for that extra wacky effect!

To make a **WIZARD'S HAT**
you will need:
Purple card * gold paper * strands of white wool * glue * scissors

1 Cut a 24-inch square from the card, and roll it into a cone shape. Make sure that the base of the cone can fit onto your head. Cut around the base of the cone to make it level.

2 Cut out moon and sun shapes from the gold paper. Glue them to the hat.

3 To make hair, glue the inside rim of the hat three-quarters of the way around, and stick the ends of the wool to it. Make sure the glue is dry before you wear the hat.

LION AND TIGER

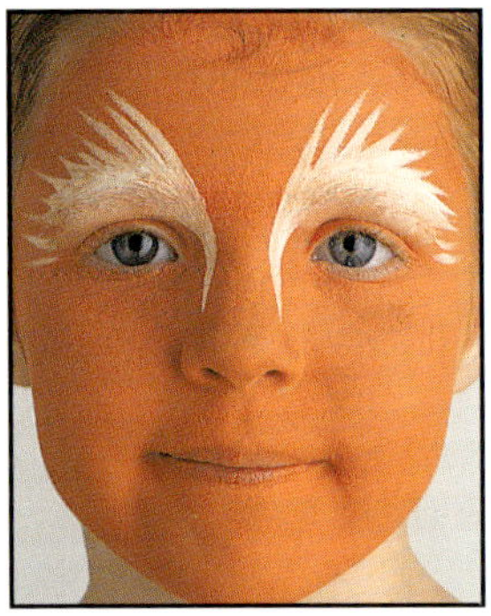

1 For the **LION**, sponge a yellow base all over the face. For the **TIGER**, apply an orange base. Paint white from the sides of the nose to over the eyelids and the eyebrows. Press very lightly on the brush as you paint over the eyebrows to give a feathery effect.

2 Using the tip of your brush, paint white stripes around the outside of the face. Paint red and black stripes between the white stripes, making sure you rinse the brush before you use a new color.

3 Paint the tip of the nose black. Then paint a black line down to the lips. Using black, outline the lips into a ferocious smile. Add little black dots for the whiskers. Finally, paint the lips red.

To make a **MANE** you will need:
Yellow and brown crêpe paper * orange and black crêpe paper * card * string * black fur fabric * glue * scissors

1 Cut a piece of card long enough to go round your head and about 4 inches wide. Cut the crêpe paper into strips as long as the card. Snip into the crêpe paper to make frills.

2 For the **LION**, glue a strip of yellow crêpe paper to the card. Glue brown crêpe paper just above this. Repeat this until the card is covered with frills. Use orange and black paper for the **TIGER**.

3 Cut out two ear shapes from the fabric and glue them to the mane. Pierce a hole in both ends of the card. Thread string through each hole to fasten the mane under the chin.

SPACE ROBOT

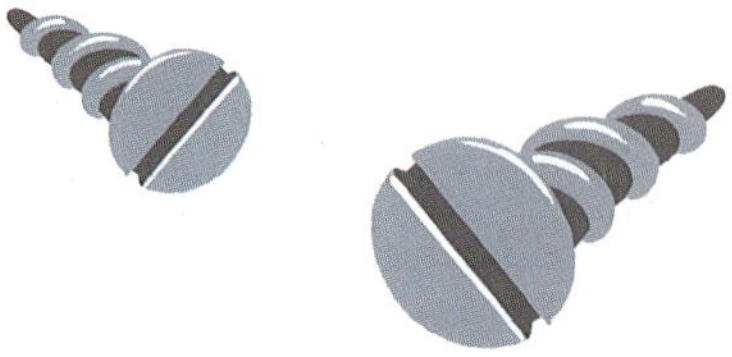

1 Apply a gray base. Add a little silver face paint if you have it for an extra metallic effect. Paint a black square around each eye and a conical shape onto the cheeks.

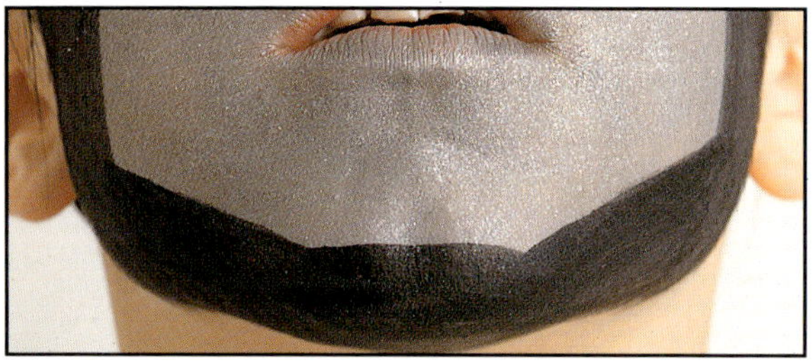

2 Using black, outline an angled shape onto the jaw bones and the chin. Fill in the color beneath the outline.

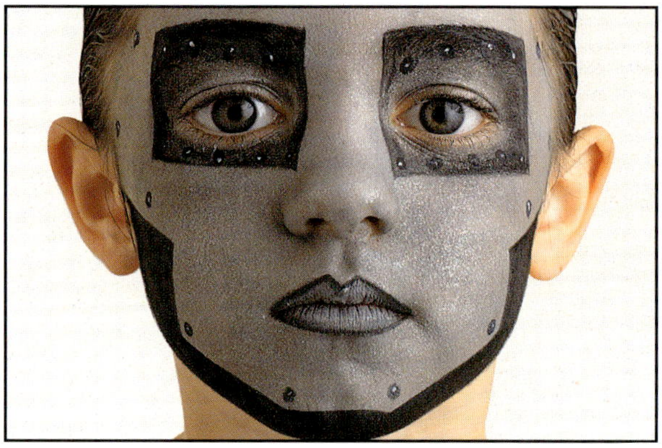

3 Add screws to the **ROBOT'S** face by painting dark gray circles with white dots around the eyes and face. Outline the lips with black.

GALACTIC WARRIOR

1 Sponge a white base all over the face. Paint purple over the eyelids, blending it to the side of the face. Paint orange above the purple, covering the eyebrows.

2 Blend green under the cheek bones. Paint pointed black eyebrows above the orange sections.

3 Paint the lips bright red and then outline them with purple. Add green dots to the orange paint.

To complete the effect, you could color the hair of your robot and warrior, and even paint their hands.

CRAFTY CAT

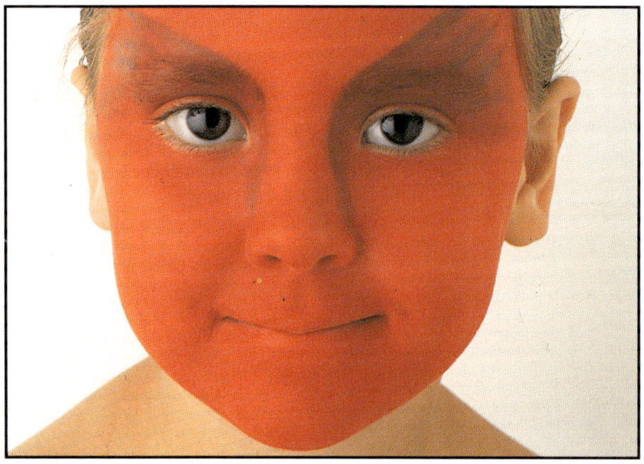

1 Sponge a red base onto the face. Blend dark red from the sides of the nose to the eyelids.

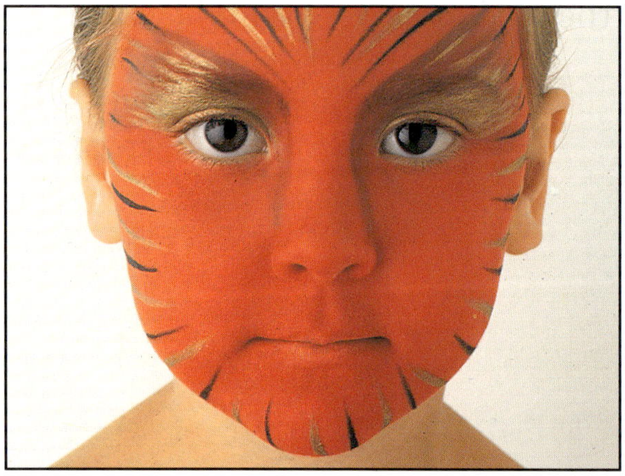

2 Paint gold, or yellow if you have no gold, over the eyelids. Paint gold, or yellow, stripes around the outside of the face, and black stripes between the gold, or yellow, stripes.

3 Carefully paint a black line under and above each eye. Paint the lips dark red. Paint the end of the nose black and then paint a black line from the nose to the lips. Still using black, add whisker dots, and outline the lips into a crafty smile.

CHEEKY MOUSE

COLOR MIX

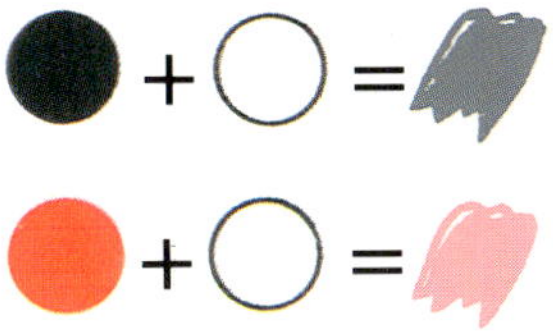

1 Sponge a gray base all over the face. Using a dry sponge, blend white above the top lip and over the nose. Paint the end of the nose pink.

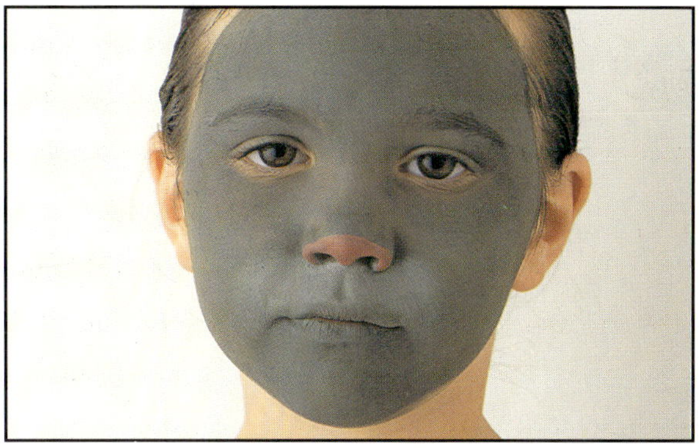

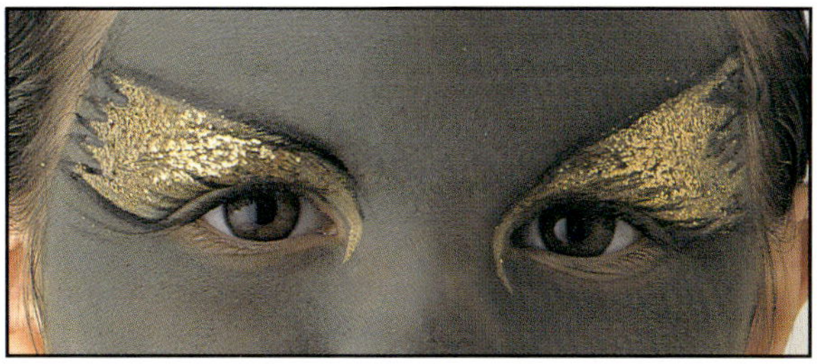

2 Cover the eyelids with gold glitter, or yellow paint. Outline the gold, or yellow, with black.

3 Paint the lips pink. Paint in a curly mouth and whiskers.

To make ears, follow the steps on page 25 using black fabric, and triangular ear shapes for the cat. Glue gold glitter to the mouse's ears.

MAGICAL MERMAID

1 Sponge a cream base lightly onto the face. Paint a turquoise wave under the cheek bones. Smudge the outline of the waves with a dry sponge.

2 Paint dark green over the eyelids, and a turquoise wave over each eyebrow. Blend the two colors together. Underline the eyes with dark green.

To make a **MERMAID COMB** you will need:
Plastic hair comb * sea-shells * poster paints * green and silver glitter * model-railway moss, or pieces of old sponge * glue

1 Glue the sea-shells and moss onto the comb.

2 Mix together different colored greens. Add a small amount of silver paint to give the colors a metallic finish. Now paint the shells and moss.

3 While the paint is still wet, sprinkle some green and silver glitter onto the shells to make them sparkle.

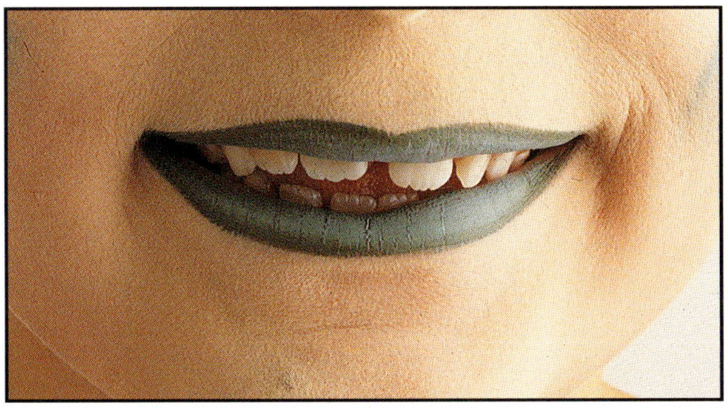

3 Paint the lips a pale turquoise and outline them with dark green. Then blend the two colors together.

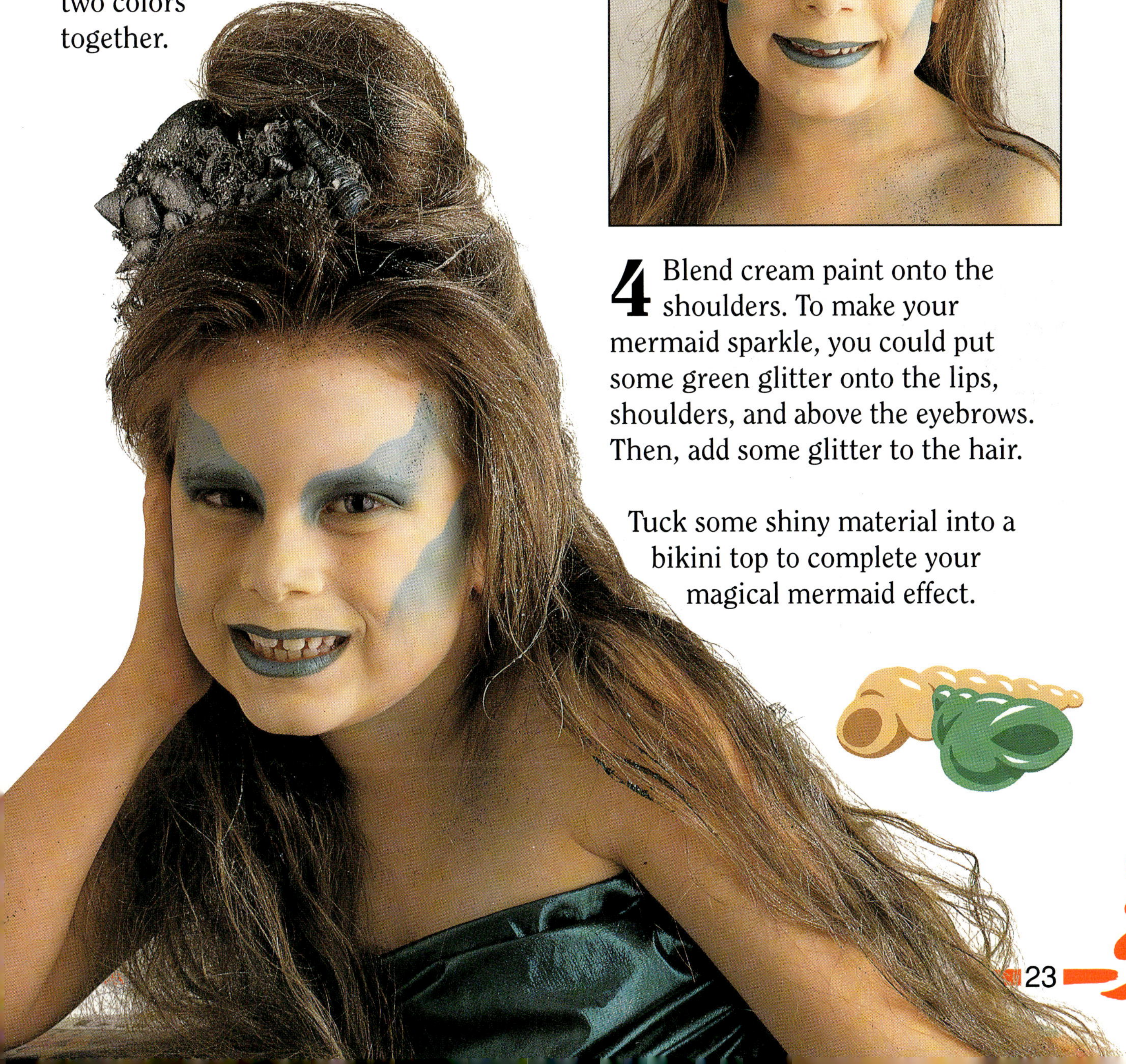

4 Blend cream paint onto the shoulders. To make your mermaid sparkle, you could put some green glitter onto the lips, shoulders, and above the eyebrows. Then, add some glitter to the hair.

Tuck some shiny material into a bikini top to complete your magical mermaid effect.

CUDDLY BEARS

COLOR MIX

PINK BEAR

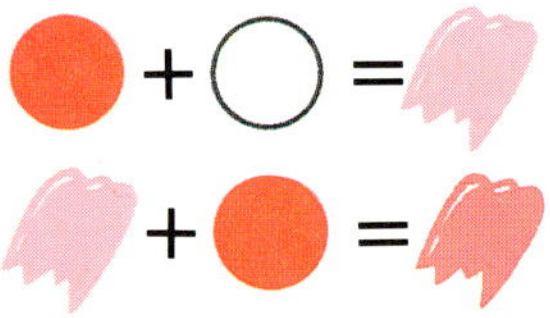

BROWN BEAR

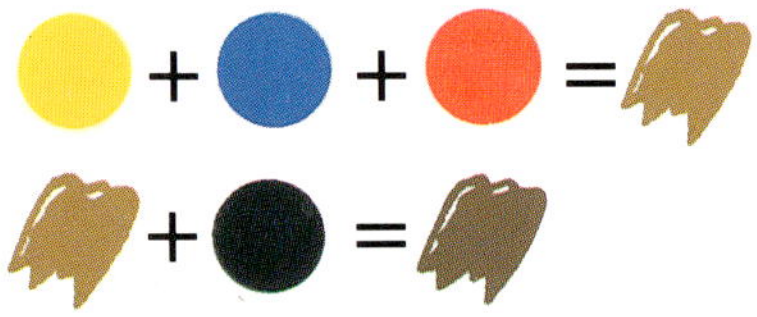

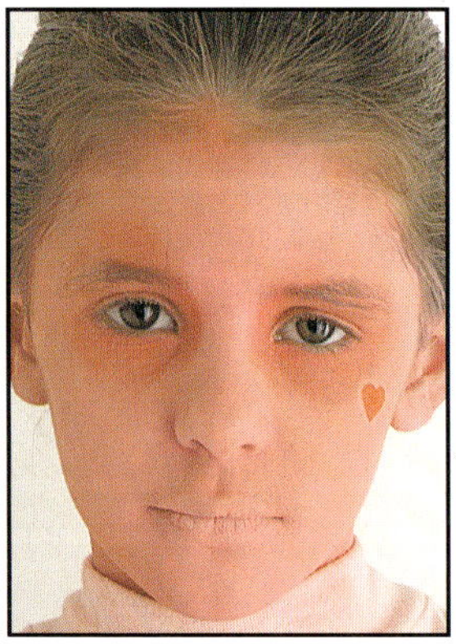

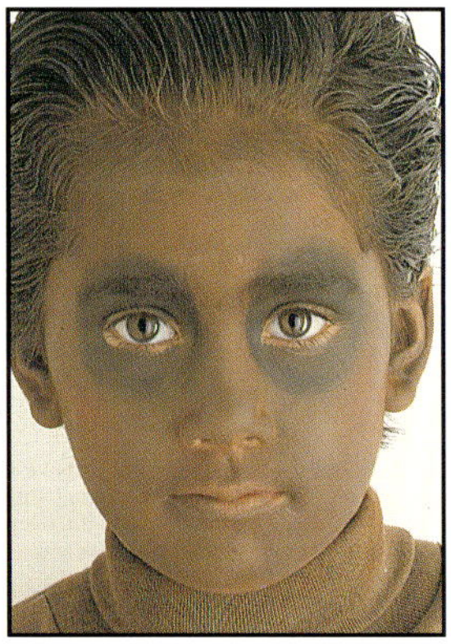

1 For the **PINK BEAR**, apply a pink base. Using the sponge, dab dark pink around the eyes. Paint a red heart onto the cheek. For the **BROWN BEAR**, apply a brown base. Using the sponge, dab dark brown around the eyes. Dampen the sponge, and dab red onto the cheeks.

To make **BEAR EARS** you will need:
Pink fur fabric * brown fur fabric * toy stuffing * headband * scissors * needle * thread

1 Cut out four circles from the fabric, each 3 inches across.

2 Place the furry sides of two of the circles towards each other. Stitch the circles together, leaving a gap of 2 inches. Repeat this with the remaining pair.

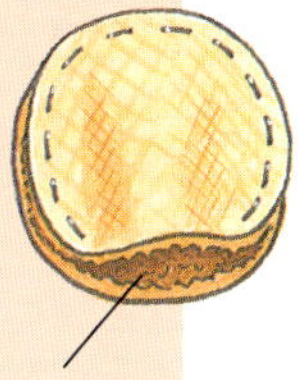

3 Turn the furry side of the ears out, and fill the ears with stuffing. Where you have left the gap, wrap either side of the fabric around the headband. Sew the gap together underneath the headband.

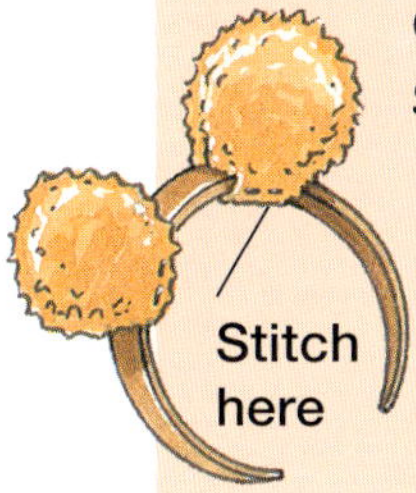

2 Paint the nose black. Using the tip of your brush, paint on black dots for the whiskers, and then a cuddly smile and two small black eyebrows.

You could color the bears' hair to match their faces.

SAD AND HAPPY CLOWNS

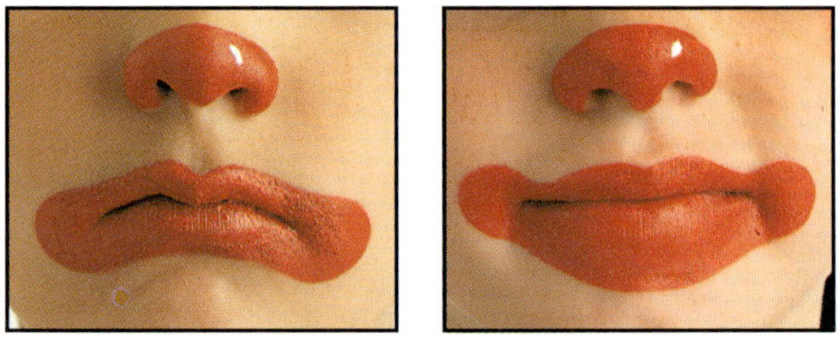

2 Using red, paint on a miserable mouth for the **SAD CLOWN**, and a smiley mouth for the **HAPPY CLOWN**. Paint the nose red, and add a white dot to its tip.

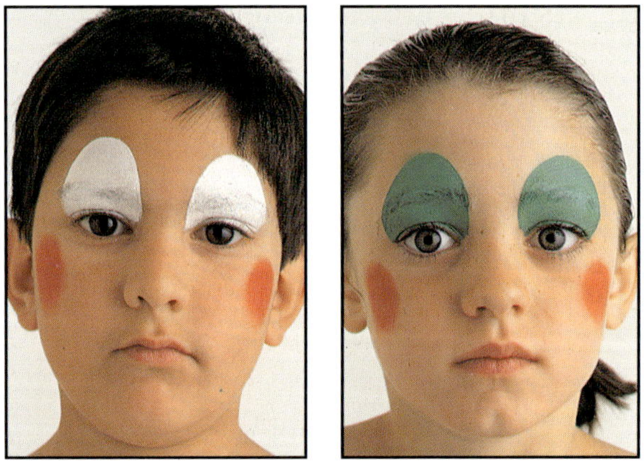

1 Using a slightly damp sponge, dab red onto the cheeks. Paint an arch over each eye, covering the eyebrows. Use white for the **SAD CLOWN**, and green for the **HAPPY CLOWN**.

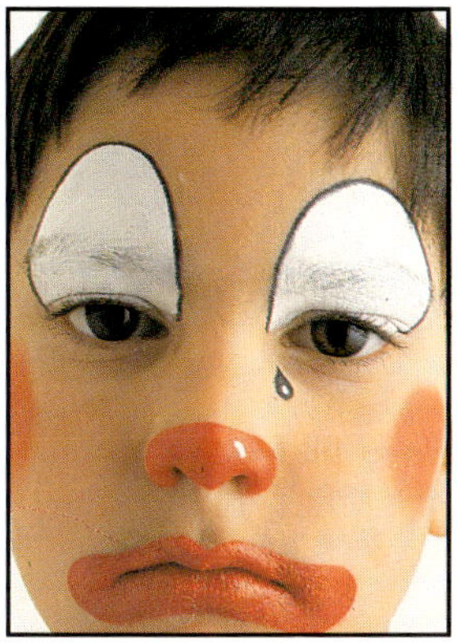

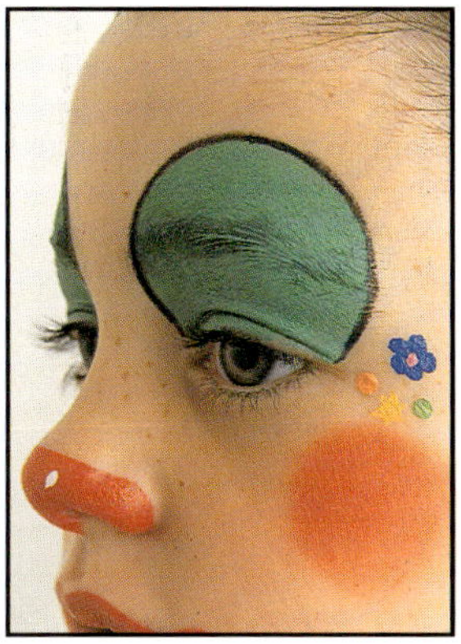

3 Outline the arches with black paint. For the **SAD CLOWN**, paint a black tear drop below the eye with a white dot in the middle of it. For the **HAPPY CLOWN**, paint brightly colored dots, stars and flowers onto the side of the face. You could use the colors shown here, or mix some of your own.

To make a **CLOWN'S FLOWER**
you will need:
Card * red, yellow and green pieces of felt * scissors * pin * elastic * needle * thread * glue * scissors

1 To make a stencil for your flower, draw a flower shape onto a piece of card and cut it out. Now draw a smaller flower shape onto some card and cut it out.

2 Pin the larger flower shape onto the yellow felt. Cut around it. Pin the smaller flower shape to the red felt, and cut around it. Unpin the card from the felt.

3 Glue the red felt flower to the yellow felt flower. Stick a dot of green felt in the middle of the red flower. Stitch both ends of the elastic to the back of the flower so that you can wear it around your neck.

SPOOKY CASTLE

COLOR MIX

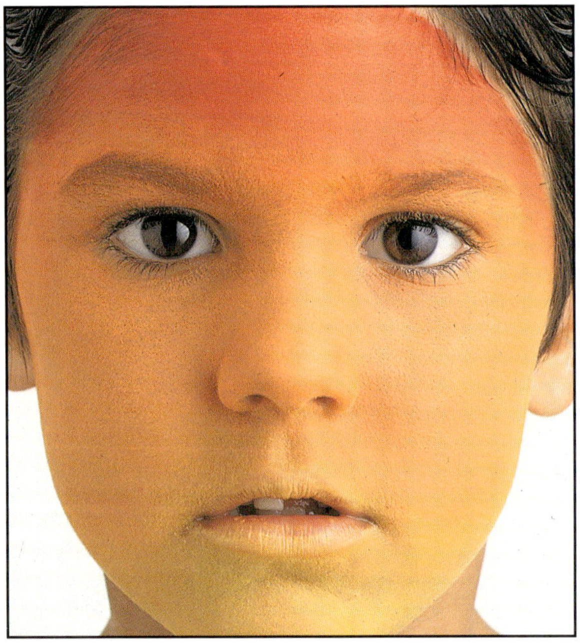

1 Apply a red base to the forehead. Add orange to the middle of the face and yellow to the chin area. Blend each color into the next with a slightly damp sponge.

2 Using black, paint a gate on one side of the chin and outline a pathway from the gate going up the cheek. Paint mountains and trees on either side of the pathway.

3 At the top of the pathway, paint in a castle with turrets and windows. Make sure that the orange base shows through the windows.

4 Paint a white moon onto the forehead, and black bats around the castle.

Make your spooky castle even more mysterious by wrapping black material around the face.

PUPPET THEATER

Face painting need not be kept just to the face. By using a cardboard grocery box and painting your fingers, you can make your own **PUPPET THEATER**. Choose your favorite story, play or pantomime, or even write your own. Paint the faces of the characters in your play onto your fingertips. Use a small piece of sponge to apply the base color, and the tip of your brush to paint the faces. You could make hats and costumes from odd bits of fabric. Follow the steps below to make a theater. When everything is ready, invite your audience to come and watch. You could use a cassette recorder for background music.

To make a **PUPPET THEATER** you will need:
Cardboard box * black paint or black felt * red velvet * gold cord * brightly colored card * gold paper * drawing pins * scissors * glue

1 Turn the box so that you can put your hand into it from underneath. Cut a rectangle out of one of the wider sides. Paint the box black or cover it with black felt.

2 Cover the back of the box with brightly colored paper. Alternatively, you could paint a scene onto a piece of paper and pin it to the back of the box.

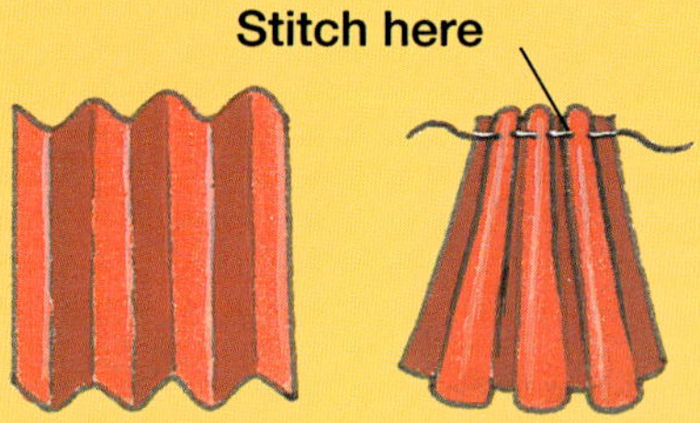

3 To make curtains, cut out two rectangles from the velvet, each as high as the box and half as wide. Fold the velvet into pleats. Stitch through the pleats to hold them in place.

4 Glue the curtains inside the box. Wrap gold cord around the curtains, gluing the ends of the cord to the inside of the box. Decorate the theater with gold cord, and masks cut out from gold paper.

FUN IDEAS

Here are some ideas for body-art. You could use these ideas to paint accessories to go with the faces and costumes in this book.

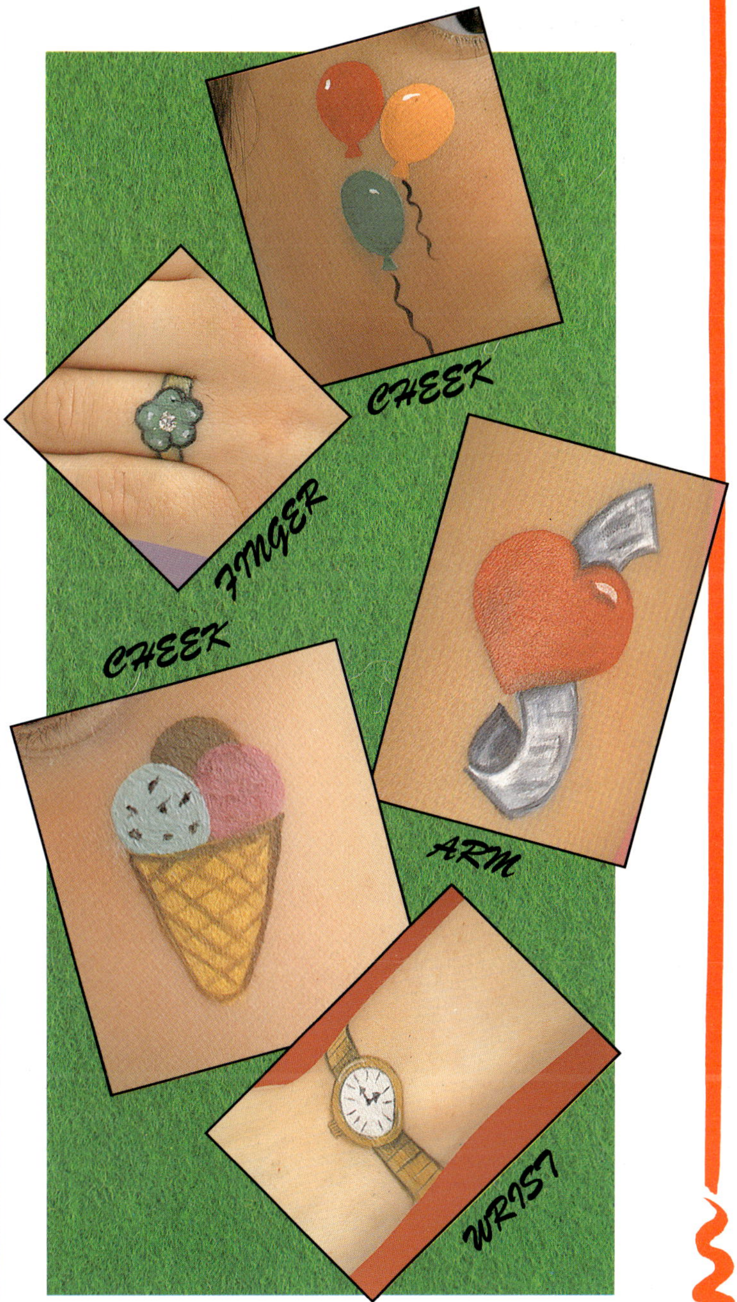

DESIGN YOUR OWN FACE

Now you have seen lots of ideas in this book, you could try painting your own designs. First of all, think of a design you would like to paint. You could look through books or photographs for ideas. Trace the outline face drawing shown here onto a piece of paper. Draw the shapes and colors you would like to use onto the outline you have traced. When you are happy with your design, try painting it onto a friend's face. Remember to start with the base color if you are using one.

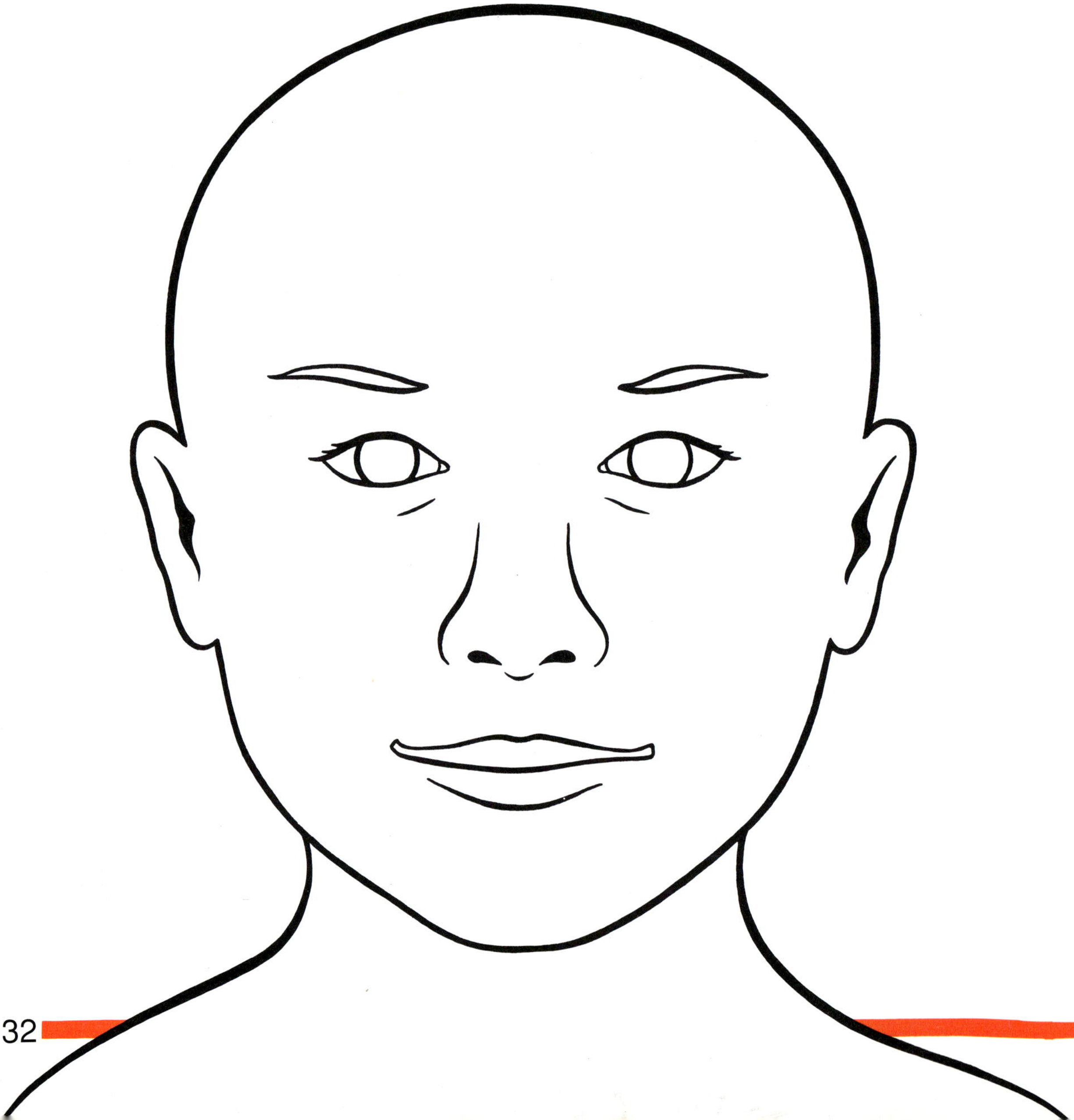